W9-AMN-797

EAU CLAIRE DISTRICT LIBRARY

T 154706

just believe

JUSTIN
BIEBER

By Riley Brooks

SCHOLASTIC INC.

Front Cover: © Newscom
Back Cover: © Getty Images

Interior: Title page: © AP Images; Page 4: © AP Images; Page 8: © Getty Images; Page 11: © AP Images; Page 13: © Getty Images; Page 14: © AP Images; Page 17: © Getty Images/WireImage; Page 18: © Getty Images/WireImage; Page 21: © Getty Images; Page 22: © Getty Images; Page 25: © AP Images; Page 26: © AP Images; Page 29: © AP Images

No part of this publication may be reproduced, stored in a retrieval system, or transmitted in any form or by any means, electronic, mechanical, photocopying, recording, or otherwise, without written permission of the publisher. For information regarding permission, write to Scholastic Inc., Attention: Permissions Department, 557 Broadway, New York, NY 10012.

ISBN 978-0-545-49454-0

All rights reserved. Published by Scholastic Inc.

SCHOLASTIC and associated logos are trademarks and/or registered trademarks of Scholastic Inc.

12 11 10 9 8 7 6 5 4 3 2 1   12 13 14 15 16 17/0
Printed in the U.S.A   40
First printing, September 2012

CONTENTS

Justin Bieber is one the hottest singers and dancers in the world. He has released multiple platinum albums, has sold out stadiums around the globe, and has shattered several music records.

While he may be an international pop sensation with seriously smooth dance moves, Justin is also a teenage guy who likes to spend time with his friends and family. So how did the Canadian cutie rise to stardom? Read on to find out!

CHAPTER 1

BABY BIEBER

Justin was born on March 1, 1994, to proud parents Pattie Mallette and Jeremy Bieber outside of Ontario, Canada. Justin's parents got divorced when he was little, but they have both always been very supportive of him.

Justin grew up in a small town called Stratford with his mom. Justin went to elementary school at Downie Central Public School and middle school at Avon Public School. He loved playing soccer in the park and hockey at the local rink with his friends. But his mom always had a feeling that music might be Justin's true calling.

When Justin was just four years old he learned to play the drums. Encouraged by his natural musical abilities, Pattie also bought him a keyboard and a guitar. "When he was five, he'd hear something on the radio and go to the keyboard and figure it out," Justin's mom explained to *Entertainment Weekly*.

Unfortunately, things weren't always so easy for Justin. Justin's mom had a hard time finding a good job. She worked two jobs and studied web design at night. Now, thanks to Justin's huge success, he can help others in need.

CHAPTER 2
FROM YOUTUBE
TO RECORD DEAL

Justin's love of music really took off when he was in seventh grade. Twelve-year-old Justin entered a local singing competition called Stratford Idol. "The other people in the competition had been taking singing lessons and had vocal coaches. I wasn't taking it too seriously at the time, I would just sing around the house," Justin explained on JustinBieberMusic.com. He didn't even practice before the competition! "It was nothing huge. I just thought it would be fun," Justin told *Entertainment Weekly*. He won second place for his performance of Matchbox Twenty's "3 AM."

Justin's family was super-proud of his accomplishment. But a few of them missed the show. So Justin posted a video of his performance on YouTube. Unexpectedly, a lot of YouTube surfers stumbled upon his video and left comments. So Justin posted more videos of himself performing covers of his favorite songs. Before long, Justin's videos had over 55 million views.

Scooter Braun, a music manager, saw Justin's videos and tracked him down. He convinced Justin to hire him as his manager. Justin didn't know it at the time, but signing with Scooter was his first step on the road to becoming a pop superstar.

As soon as the ink was dry on Justin's contract, Scooter landed Justin a record deal with Island Def Jam Records in a deal headed up by CEO Antonio "L.A." Reid and Usher.

Usher stepped up to guide Justin. "He was an amazing talent and find. Given my experience, I knew exactly what it would take for him to become an incredible artist," Usher told Reuters.com. Like Justin, Usher signed his first record deal at age thirteen, so he knew how to guide the young star. "[Usher] just basically told me to keep my head on straight. Make sure to stay grounded," Justin explained to NeonLimelight.com. Justin was lucky to have such a successful recording artist be his mentor!

CHAPTER 3
MY WORLD

Justin's debut album, *My World,* was everything he wanted it to be, and his YouTube fans loved it, too. All four singles from *My World* were Top 15 hits in Canada and Top 40 hits in the U.S. Justin is the only artist in history to have four singles from a debut album in the Top 40 before the album's release. So when *My World* finally hit store shelves on November 17, 2009, it was no surprise that it was an immediate success!

Once his album released, Justin started recording music videos. You'd think Justin would have already been a video pro since his career started on YouTube, but making a professional music video was a big change!

"It was really different going from a video camera to a professional camera. It was really crazy, but it was an amazing experience," Justin explained to Billboard.com. Luckily for his fans, Justin was a natural in his music videos and looked even cuter than he did on YouTube!

EAU CLAIRE DISTRICT LIBRARY

CHAPTER 4

BIEBER FEVER

Less than four months after *My World* hit store shelves, Justin released *My World 2.0* on March 19, 2010. It was a difficult schedule for Justin, but the hard work was worth it for his fans.

My World 2.0 debuted at number one on the U.S. Billboard 200. That made Justin the youngest solo male act to top the chart since Stevie Wonder in 1963. When *My World 2.0* sold more copies in its second week than it had in the first week, Justin set a world record—as the first musical act since The Beatles to debut at number one and then sell more copies the following week. It was a big honor to Justin to break records set by two legendary musical acts!

Justin promoted his newest album with lots of radio interviews, photo shoots, new music videos, and big performances at major Hollywood events.

Then, for Thanksgiving 2010, Justin released *My Worlds Acoustic,* an entirely acoustic album featuring his top hits from *My World* and *My World 2.0.* It was the perfect Christmas gift for Bieber fans everywhere— especially since it included a brand-new song called "Pray," which fans loved!

After releasing his first two albums, Justin launched his *My World* Tour in June 2010. Justin loved being on tour—he got to meet his fans, explore new cities, and rock out in huge stadiums. Justin even got to perform in some of the most famous venues of all time, like Madison Square Garden. That was a pretty big deal for Justin, since, until he signed with Scooter, he'd never been outside of Canada!

Of course, being on the road nonstop wasn't always easy. Traveling can be very exhausting, and Justin missed his family and friends. But it was all worth it, since it meant so much to his fans to see him live.

Justin performed his last show of the tour in October 2011 after a year and a half of touring. The tour was a hit with fans—selling more than 1.3 million tickets overall. It seemed like the entire world had caught Bieber Fever!

When Justin did take the occasional break from touring in 2010, he stayed plenty busy guest starring and performing on popular TV shows like *My Date With . . .* and *True Jackson, VP.*

On April 10, 2010, Justin was the musical guest on *Saturday Night Live.* Then Justin guest starred in the season premiere of *CSI: Crime Scene Investigation.* It was his first time playing a dramatic role, and Justin was a natural.

Justin made his move to the big screen on February 11, 2011, with his 3-D movie *Justin Bieber: Never Say Never,* which featured concert footage and exclusive behind-the-scenes footage from Justin's *My World* Tour. Justin loved that all of his fans who weren't able to see him live could experience him in concert through the film.

And in early 2012 Justin surprised everyone when he made an appearance at the Academy Awards with host Billy Crystal. Justin got a lot of laughs from the audience and looked supercute in his tux!

The year 2012 also marked the premiere of the newest version of MTV's *Punk'd*, which features a different young celebrity host each week. Justin was picked to be the host of the premiere episode! Justin had a great time filming the show and got Taylor Swift good when he made her think that she had blown up a boat rented by a wedding party! Justin's fans loved seeing him on TV, but what they really wanted was more music—and Justin couldn't wait to give it to them!

CHAPTER 6
UNDER THE MISTLETOE

Justin loves Christmas—it's his favorite holiday! "I love Christmas, being with my family up in Canada," Justin told *USA Today*. "To me, Christmas is about giving." So, in 2011, Justin decided to give his fans the ultimate Christmas present: his brand-new holiday album called *Under the Mistletoe*. He partnered with Sean Kingston, Taylor Swift, and others to record a mix of Christmas classics like "All I Want for Christmas is You" and "Silent Night," and new, soon-to-be-classic holiday songs like "Home This Christmas."

One of Justin's favorite songs from the album was "Mistletoe," and he made sure he had an awesome music video to go with it! "I'm really excited. [The song is] really catchy. I know all my fans are going to love it. It's something that I feel like they're going to be singing every Christmas," Justin told *MTV News*. Filmed in Franklin, Tennessee, the video featured Justin on a date with a pretty brunette actress. It was a very sweet video, and very festive!

Under the Mistletoe was the first Christmas album by a male artist to ever debut at number one when it hit store shelves on November 1, 2011. Justin's holiday album definitely got his fans into the Christmas spirit, and true Bieber fans keep those songs playing on their iPods year-round.

CHAPTER 7
BEHIND THE SCENES

So what's life like off-screen for pop's hottest star? Justin and his mom spend most of their time in Los Angeles. Justin misses being close to his father and friends in Canada, but he keeps in touch with plenty of calls, e-mails, and visits.

Justin loves spending time with his friends and fellow celebs when he's not working, including Taylor Swift, Ashley Tisdale, Samantha Droke, Martin Johnson, and Logan Henderson, Kendall Schmidt and Carlos Pena from Big Time Rush. Justin and his friends even filmed an unofficial music video for up-and-coming singer Carly Rae Jepsen's single, "Call Me Maybe."

He loves grabbing lunch, hitting the beach, or hanging out and making funny videos with his buds. Justin is also notorious for pulling pranks, so his friends are always on guard around him!

Justin also finds plenty of time to spend with Selena Gomez, his girlfriend and best friend. The two have gone on vacations together and have been spotted all over L.A. on romantic dates. Once Justin rented out a huge arena in L.A. so that he and Selena could watch the movie *Titanic* on the big screen—too cute! The couple attended the 2011 Vanity Fair Oscar Party, which they joked was their version of prom.

Selena was right by Justin's side all night at his star-studded surprise 18th birthday party at the Beverly Wilshire Hotel. There were even performances from Carly Rae Jepsen and Taio Cruz! It was definitely a night to remember for Justin!

But Justin's favorite part about stardom is getting to meet and inspire his fans. "I'm looking forward to influencing others in a positive way," Justin explained on JustinBieberMusic.com. "My message is you can do anything if you just put your mind to it." Justin's success is constantly inspiring his fans around the world!

So what's next for J.B.? He's been busy recording his newest album, *Believe*. His first single from the album, "Boyfriend," was released in March 2012 and fans loved it. Justin collaborated with a lot of artists, including Kanye West and Drake, for his newest songs. "This new album is crazy. I've spent the most time on it creatively just writing myself and being involved in the whole process. It's something that comes from my heart," Justin told MTV.com.

As much as Justin loves performing, he is also interested in the business side of music. His manager, Scooter Braun, has allowed

Justin to learn the ropes at his record label, Schoolboy Records. Justin recently helped Scooter sign Canadian singer Carly Rae Jepsen, and is dedicated to signing more Canadian talent to his manager's label.

Despite his busy schedule, Justin has found time to give back to his fans and to causes around the world, like spending time with a six-year-old superfan battling cancer, and telling fans to donate to charity (helping poor countries build wells for clean water) instead of sending him birthday gifts for the past two years. Working to make the world a better place is very important to Justin and he is dedicated to giving back as much as possible whenever he can!

Justin's career is super-hot and he has the drive every star needs to stay in the spotlight for a long time. So stay tuned: Justin will be very busy over the next few years.

CHAPTER 9

JUST THE FACTS

Name: **Justin Drew Bieber**

Nicknames: **JBiebs, Beebs**

Birthday: **March 1, 1994**

Hometown: **Ontario, Canada**

Current Town: **Los Angeles, California**

Pet: **dogs named Sam and Baylor**

Siblings: **half sister Jazmyn and half brother Jaxon**

Hobbies: **hockey, pulling pranks, making funny videos**

Favorite Color: **purple**

Favorite Foods: **spaghetti and meatballs, tacos**

Favorite Number: **6**

Favorite Drink: **orange juice**

Favorite Movies: **the Rocky series**

Favorite Dessert: **apple pie**